When the "Vow" Breaks

Terry Nunn

When the "Vow" Breaks

Published and distributed by Terry Nunn Publishing

Maplewood, NJ

Printed and bound in the United States of America.

Edited by Katherine Washington

Cover created by Blue Screen Graphic Design Studio, LLC

Author's photo by Shaquana Leverett

Publisher's Note

ISBN 978-0-692-84138-9

First Print February 2017

DEDICATIONS

First and foremost, I would like to thank God. Without Him, none of this would be possible. I thank my family for being there for me. I have a great support team behind me. To my brother, Marcus and my sisters Pookie and Pam, thank you for holding me down in my time of need. To my Mom and Pops, thank you for your support as well. To my two beautiful children, thank you for being with me through all the stress and pain. Also, I'd like to thank my favorite cousin, Mr. Austin, for always being in my corner no matter what. I send a shout out to my entire family and true friends who helped me get though some of the roughest times in my life and were always there for me during my time of need. To all those who have been with me through my ups and downs, I thank you. And to my good friend KB, who picked my head up and made me smile again…Thanks for that. For all of those that I may have missed, blame it on my head, not my heart! God bless you all!

Introduction

My name is Gene Terry Nunn. I began writing this project knowing that I may be judged. Judged because of my love for someone who didn't love me back. I know people will call me dumb, stupid, a moron and other words like that, but none of that matters to me. I am telling my story, to help other people who may be going through the same thing I am going through. Men normally take secrets such as these to their grave, but I'm different. When I decided to get married, I did so with the belief that my marriage would last forever, but what do you do when the "vow" breaks…

Introducing **PART 1-Chapter 1…In the Beginning**

One thing we all have in common is, we were all born of a mother. We were all created by a sperm and an egg meeting. How they may have come to meet, might be different but the result of that sperm and that egg meeting is human life. So listen, I was born in 1976. A healthy, beautiful baby boy, by the name of Gene Terry Nunn. My parents Peggy and Gene Nunn doted on their curly haired son.

I had a normal childhood. Or one that was normal to me. My parents were loving parents, married. Protectors and providers. They both worked hard and we had a nice home. We had everything we needed, wanted and could ask for.

Our childhood is a part of what shapes us and determines who we are to become as adults. As I grew up I saw my parents as a happy, married couple, who rarely argued, and I'd never seen them fight. This is what my normal was. In my mind, this same scenario was being replayed in every household in America.

My mother had 2 daughters when she met my father. He had a son. They came together as a family and embraced each other's children from previous relationships. They got married and then me and my brother came along. As a child, I didn't really understand who had what, or whose kids were whose, all I knew was that these were my siblings. We were all loved together and got in trouble together. Our bond was formed as siblings and nobody was concerned whether we were half, whole or steps. We were just brothers and sisters who loved each other, had fun together and had each other's back and held each other down. That closeness continues even to this day.

It was not until I got older and wiser that I realized that everyone is not raised the same way. Everyone is not raised with both a mother and father and they may not have siblings. The things I learned growing up were different from what others may have learned in their formative years. Since everyone's childhood experiences aren't the same, it is natural that our view of life and what it should be like will also be different. Something that is acceptable to one, might not be acceptable to another. This is not something that I was made aware of or that I can say I ever thought about as a child. I was just a kid that liked to play, have fun, do well in school and get gifts. I thought that's what life was all about.

Not until I became a pre-teen, my voice began to change, I began to get hair in places I didn't know hair was going to grow and I began to notice girls, it was then that I realized that life had a lot more to offer. You see, in my teenage years, light skin was in and if you had curly hair you could smash anything moving. Girls were attracted to me for my looks but more so, for the respectful way that I treated them. My father taught me to always respect women and to treat them how I would want my mother and sisters to be treated and I rolled with that. Women were not bitches and whores to me. They were beautiful queens and goddesses. I didn't have a type. I was a sucker for a pretty face and of course a nice body and if she smiled at me, it was on.

I remember my first girlfriend. We were both 14 and innocent. She was pretty and sweet and I loved to walk her to and from school. We started out innocently enough, showing our affection for each other with just kisses and tight hugs. I might be able to cop a feel here and there but we enjoyed our youth. I didn't check for other girls either, only her. As time went on and our feelings for one another became stronger, we decided to be each other's first. Her parents were away for the weekend and she invited me over. We were both nervous and the sex happened so quick, I didn't even know it was done. That first time, and having your first orgasm is a feeling a man chases for the rest of his life. Having sex brought us closer together. We did it anytime we could and enjoyed doing it. It was the summer of our 10th grade year that I received heartbreaking news. Unexpectedly, her parents sprang on her, that they were moving to Florida. We were young, but we had been faithful to each other, I had never betrayed her nor had she betrayed me. Just as luck would have it, she was being taken away from me and I was left alone.

I had heard of being lovesick, of others not being able to eat or sleep after a breakup, but now I was experiencing those feelings first hand. I really did feel sick, I couldn't eat or sleep. I felt like it was the end of the world for me, especially since I truly loved and cared for her. It wasn't like I couldn't get girls though, getting girls was never the problem for me. It was just that I had an intense attachment to my first girlfriend and I missed her. It wasn't long before my friends and cousins got me in that zone of, 'There are plenty of fish in the sea,' and from then on that is the mindset I was in.

It's funny how one situation in life can change who you are as a human being. I was a tad bit scared to get attached and fall in love again because I learned that in the blink of an eye, we can lose the person we love or they can just move away.

My nick name had always been T-Rex but then it changed to T-Sex because girls were throwing it at me and I was catching it at every turn. I didn't have a problem going out anywhere and leaving with someone. Short, tall, skinny, thick, light, brown…it was whatever and whoever. They became nameless, faceless creatures that I was just hitting and dismissing.

After graduating from high school, my mind was not on college, it was on girls. I went to every college party throughout New Jersey, so it felt like I went to college. My parents didn't raise me to be a knucklehead so the only thing I could do was get a job. My sister helped me get a job at her place of employment in occupational therapy. I worked there for years and during that job my life changed.

When I turned 24 and walked into Professionals, a bar on Avon Avenue and 19th Street in Newark, NJ my whole world changed. It was October 2000, and the air had that crisp fall feel. The weather wasn't cold and wasn't hot, it was comfortable. Me and my boys walked into Professionals just for a night of drinking and chilling. As we pushed our way through the open door, the bar was crowded but as I entered, she was the first person I saw, and it was as if time stood still. I was mesmerized. I felt like nobody else was in the bar but the two of us. As I stared at her my mouth probably hung open a little. It was as if cupid shot me with an arrow and a bullet.

My cousin continuously called my name and finally hit my arm and said,

"Yo T, what do you want to drink?" My mind was boggled, I said,

"Huh? Uhhh nothing. I will be right back."

She watched me as I walked over to her. She smiled and I smiled. I swallowed hard and put a little extra swag in my step because I didn't want her to think I wasn't confident in myself. She sat at the bar sipping her drink and I slowly looked her from up to down. I pulled my lip in imagining how I would punish her if I got her in my bed. She had grown up. I remembered her from the area. She was a little younger than me so she was never anyone I paid much attention to. Since I was a couple of years older, I only knew her as the little girl that lived around the way. She was now the grown woman whom I wanted to swing my way. As I reached her, I spoke first,

"Heyyyy how you doing?" She smiled and bashfully replied

"I'm okay. How are you?" I replied with my corny player line,

"Better now that I have seen you." She smiled again and we began to converse. I bought her and her friends drinks and we talked the entire time I was there. She told me she was single, had a two-year-old and was working at a pharmaceutical company. I joked,

"So, you sell drugs huh?"

She laughed and it made it easier to talk to her. She was plain but she was everything to my eyes. After some time had passed, my boys were ready to go. This was before the current era of pull out your cell phone and take the number down. This was the, get a piece of paper and write it down era. My boys were rushing me. I leaned in close and whispered in her ear,

"Let me get your number so we can finish our conversation." She wrote her number down and said,

"Don't forget to call me." I kissed her softly on her cheek and replied,

"Oh, I won't." I had had a few drinks of my own and was a little tipsy, but I held myself together long enough to fold up the piece of paper and put it in that small top pocket of my jeans. Back in the day, jeans had so many pockets. My boys and I hid the numbers we got from other females, from our girlfriends, in those small pockets at the top, but I was single and I wasn't hiding anything from anyone.

We left Professionals and went on to the next spot and then the next spot. I met random chicks at the other spots but she stayed on my mind heavy. When I finally got home and crashed, drunk off my ass, I went to sleep and I slept hard. The next day I got up and wanted to call her.

I had to think about where her number was and quickly went into the pants pocket to retrieve it. No number. I searched the other pocket, still, no number. I looked around my room for that piece of paper and couldn't find it anywhere. I threw on some sweats, ran out to my car and searched high and low, no number. I was screwed! How could I lose my destiny's phone number?! Like really, how could the only person on my brain, not be reachable?! We both discussed that we didn't live in the old neighborhood anymore, so I had no idea how to contact her. None of my boys connected with any of her girls, and I figured I had to take the loss and pray I saw her somewhere again. I knew what kind of car she drove, and I stalked Professionals for like a week to see if that was her hang out. It wasn't. I couldn't get her off my brain but realistically I had to move on. If it was meant to be, it was going to be.

Chapter 2

So a few weeks went by and it was time to do laundry. My mother raised a self-sufficient man. I knew how to cook, clean and wash my own clothes. I was sitting on my bed, separating the colors from the whites and something rolled onto the floor. I picked it up and it was like I heard the angels sing….it was her number! I forgot about the laundry and immediately called her. She answered with a slight attitude,

"Hello?" I got a bit intimidated and asked if I could speak to her. She replied,

"This is her who is this?" I put on my sexy voice,

"Terry." I heard the smile through the phone as her tone softened and she said,

"Why are you just calling me? I have been waiting by this phone for over two weeks!"

I explained to her what happened and she calmed down and we talked for hours and hours. I heard my cordless phone beeping indicating it was about to die, but I wasn't ready to hang up. I was smitten with this girl and I hadn't even smelled it yet. I hadn't even tasted the sweet kisses from her lips but I was feeling her. My phone eventually died and I had to hang up but I didn't want it to be long before I talked to or saw her again.

We spoke every day, all day, for 3 straight days and then she finally invited me over. Her daughter was there and she said,

"I have someone I want you to meet."

Her daughter was so pretty and she came right to me. I hadn't really dated girls with kids before. This was new to me but it didn't matter. I wanted this girl and her daughter to be my family. I know you're saying to yourself, 'After one date?' Yes, after one date. Which wasn't even really a date. She did cook a meal for me and I ate it all. We watched a movie and I played on the floor with her daughter and her toys. She smiled at me and I smiled back at her. It was almost like we both knew that this was going to be something special. We continued hanging out for two weeks. I had gotten a few kisses and copped some feels but I hadn't been in them walls yet. On this particular day, I thought:

'Today, is the day, I'm going over to her apartment and she is giving up them drawers'. I mean in my heart and in my eyes those drawers were going to be mine forever.

So I arrived at her place and within minutes, someone is knocking, or should I say, banging on the door. She looked at me and I looked at her. Now me, I'm a lover not a fighter but I am not a punk. I don't go around starting trouble but I don't run from it either. She looked at me and said,

"Ignore that, it's my daughter's father." The banging was becoming louder from him hitting the door so hard and he was yelling mad obscenities. The baby was crying and I was like,

"Listen, if you're going to be mine, this dude is going to have to respect that." She begged me not to open the door but I did. Her baby's father and I stood there, sizing each other up. I spoke first,

"Look man, I understand the situation. You can come see your daughter anytime but I cannot allow you to disrespect my woman in front of me."

He said something slick and she put the baby down and ran and got a butcher knife and charged after him. I held her back as he said,

"You better get that crazy bitch." I pushed her back and pulled the knife from her hands.

"Chill. Man listen, maybe it is best if you left. I just asked you not to disrespect her and I won't disrespect you in front of your daughter." I closed the door and she ran to the window. I saw him and his boys leaning on the car, I guess waiting for me. I wasn't going to walk into a war without soldiers.

I was about to make some phone calls of my own, but she cried and begged me not to saying,

"That's my daughter's father." I calmed myself down and comforted her daughter until she fell asleep. She called her mother and asked her if the baby could come to her house for the night, explaining what happened. Her mother was understanding and said yes, and the two of us went together to drop her off. We couldn't get back to her crib fast enough.

We entered her apartment and she tried to play shy but I didn't. I pushed her down on her couch and began to kiss her like she was the air I needed to breathe. I took my shirt off and continued kissing her while I helped her get out of her clothes at the same time. I went in my pocket and got a condom, carried her to her bed and punished her. I was so deep in them guts and asking her,

"Whose is this?" She kept saying,

"Yours." I looked her in her eyes,

"Say my name!" She cried out,

"Terry. It's yours." As her lips said my name it was so sexy and I pushed in so hard the condom popped. I didn't stop though. Hell, if she got pregnant we were just going to be having a baby. She told me it was mine, I told her baby's father this was my girl. I had a readymade family and I couldn't be happier about it.

After I rolled off her, she sat up and I jumped because something hairy was on the pillow. I yelled,

"Wait turn the light on…what's that?" She looked down slightly embarrassed and snatched it off the pillow.

"That's my track Negro! You laid it down so good you made my weave come out." We both had a good laugh from that. She went to her bathroom and got a nice warm wash cloth and cleaned me up as a good woman should. We laid there in each other's arms talking about our future together. The picture we painted of us together was so bright, I really needed shades. I held her and kissed her on the forehead wondering,

'*Where has she been all my life*?' I know, I was still young but I could have easily skipped the T-Sex phase. This was all the loving I ever needed. I couldn't have been happier at that moment in my life….

ISSUE # 1 LUST –

The definition of lust is: "Very strong sexual desire."

Terry's definition of lust:

I believe that lust is being attracted to the outside, or all that we can see with the physical eye. This is when a man is thinking with his little head and not his big one. It is what keeps a man attracted and involved and the sex going every day. Lust. Without it, today we might not ever get to the love. It's true that we have to be attracted to someone first to even know if we want to proceed and find out more or move on to someone else. . At my age now, I know this is not true. A man can fall in love with someone without ever lusting after them. My issue was, I allowed my lust to lead me into love, with blinders on. I was blind then, but now I can see. This is my story…

Chapter 3

We enjoyed 3 days of good love making and I finally went back to my own home. I was walking around in bliss…That was until one morning I had to take a piss. I stood at the toilet and it felt funny. I began to pee and it was like fire shot out of my dick. I screamed out in pain and looked at my boxers. There was puss in them. What the hell was this? I didn't know what to do. I stuck my manhood in the sink and began to wash it really good. I squeezed the head and puss was coming out. I thought I was going to die. I didn't know what was going on. I hadn't been with anyone in weeks except…. how could the girl I was basically falling in love with give me an STD?! This couldn't be right. I called my cousin Fred, aka Mr. Austin, because he was older and I trusted him with any and every one of my secrets. He laughed a bit at my panic.

"Well it seems you got burnt my dude. Who you been fucking raw." I thought back to the night the condom broke and I didn't stop. The other nights I still wore a condom but that first night when it broke, it was so wet, so good and so mine I didn't stop. Fred told me,

"Look you're going to have to go to the clinic. DO NOT GO TO THE CLINIC IN DOWNTOWN NEWARK!" Still naïve about these things, I asked,

"Why not?"

Fred replied,

"Do you want all of Newark in your business? Go to another town like Clifton or somewhere."

I took his advice. I had Chlamydia. The clinic told me that it takes about 3 days for a man to see signs of chlamydia and it was right on time. The thing is, a female might not have any signs at all. I had so many mixed emotions, I didn't know what to do. The doctor told me if I wore a condom, I couldn't give it to anyone.

I continued to see her and she kept trying to get at me for sex. I made up every excuse in the world why we couldn't. I had a headache. I hurt my back at work. I was too tired... She finally came to me one day crying, and asking,

"Who is she?" I asked her,

"Who is who?" She replied,

"Who is she that's got you not wanting to have sex with me?!" I had to tell her.

"Yo, I didn't want to tell you but I was diagnosed with Chlamydia." Her eyes got big.

"What? Did you give it to me?" I was offended.

"No! You gave it to me! I haven't been with anybody since the day I met you." She cried into her hands.

"How can this be? Oh, my God, I am so sorry. If I gave it to you I didn't know I had it!" I comforted her and kissed her on the forehead.

"Yeah, the doctor said most women don't have any signs, but a man can have signs as early as 3 days later. I didn't know how to tell you, but now that you know, you need to make a doctor's appointment."

She agreed and the next day we went to the doctor together. I forgave her for this issue but little did I know, there was going to be a lot more forgiving coming from my end.... Pay attention.

ISSUE #2 TRUST -

The definition of trust is: "Firm belief in the reliability, truth, ability, or strength of someone or something."

Terry's definition of Trust:

For me, trust is when I believe in and/or see nothing wrong with anything a person does. Trust is what helps a relationship go a long way. Their word is their bond and my bond with them allows me to believe everything they say. Whatever that person says, I don't second guess or question it. I believe it because I trust them. We can become almost gullible and naive about that person because what they tell us is the law. What others see or feel don't matter, only what we have with that person and how we feel about each other matters…

Chapter 4

So after we got past that hurdle, we moved in together. She and her daughter moved with me into my one bedroom apartment on 15th Street in Newark. The street address is not important, but the location is. This story is about how money makes all things change in your life, even your address.

We were the perfect little family. My older sister moved into her apartment so that she wouldn't lose her deposit or be charged for breaking her lease. When the lease was up my sister decided to move. We decided that her old apartment on Munn Street, in East Orange was safer than 15th Street in Newark, so we moved back. I was in love and this is one of the things that love made a man do. It made me want to keep my family safe.

I had been in love before but never like this, this was, what I perceived to be the real thing. We talked about God and decided to join a church. We joined a church together as one. After that, it made sense to just go ahead and take the plunge by asking her to marry me. I called Fred, my number one cousin on earth. I told Fred,

"This is it. She is the one. I want to marry her." Fred asked,

"Are you sure man? You are still young and there are a lot of fish in the sea." I laughed and assured him she was the one. He gave me his blessing and off I went to find the perfect ring.

I headed to Jersey Garden Mall with my boys, the Twins, Roc and Kerm, in tow. They were younger than me but they were like "go for it." They both agreed that it wasn't something they were ready to do but they gave me their blessing. We went to the jewelry counter and looked for rings. I looked and looked until I found what I thought was the perfect one that she would love. Now bear with me, I was only 23 years old. Still a baby in today's society's eyes. I picked out a ring and the salesmen told me,

"$1,500." The Twins both said,

"Hell no, that's too much." I laughed,

"Nope this is the one."

Nothing was too good for my girl. I put $1,000 of my hard-earned working man's money down. I don't have stories of when I used to hustle. I was always the hard-working pretty boy. I came home happy and excited. Couldn't wait to get up the other $500 and make this official. I walked around on cloud nine. I worked overtime to hustle that money up. I couldn't get to the mall fast enough to get the ring off layaway. When I came home her daughter was with her mother and I told her to get dressed. I began to drive and looked over at her in the passenger seat of my car. She looked beautiful to me. Just perfect. I began to get a little emotional and asked,

"Yo, do you love me?" She was taken aback and said,

"Of course, I do. Why did you ask me that?" I replied,

"You sure yo? You sure you love me?" She began to get nervous.

"I said yes I do, why are you asking me that? What is wrong with you?" I said,

"I'm just asking…So you rocking with me, like for real or is this a game?" She then started to get annoyed at my line of questions.

"What are you talking about? Of course, I am rocking with you. You are making me nervous." I pulled into Weequahic Park because this proposal had to happen now. I wanted to do it on one knee in a restaurant but my mind couldn't wait. I pulled over and stopped the car. I turned in my seat and faced her. I asked one last time,

"You sure you love me?" She turned in her seat and looked me dead in my eyes.

"YES, TERRY I AM SURE." I broke out in my infamous smile while pulling out the ring and asked,

"Well will you marry me?" Her eyes got the size of golf balls. She covered her mouth and looked at the ring and then at me. She grabbed it and pushed it on her finger.

"Of course, I will. I love you Terry." She jumped across the car and into my arms. She kissed me and then held on and hugged me. I hugged her back. This was going to be my wife. She pulled back from our embrace with tears in her eyes. Her tears brought tears to my eyes. She kissed me again on my cheek.

"Thank you, Terry. You have made me the happiest woman on earth. I can't wait to spend the rest of my life with you." That line alone made my heart smile and my senses crumble. I was so weak for this girl that anything she said, I believed.

She began to call all her friends and I could hear that some sounded really happy for her and others not so much, they sounded like they were faking it. I could hear the jealousy in some of their voices but I didn't care. I wanted her to be happy and I thought she was…

PART 2

LOVE...

The definition of love is: "An intense feeling of deep affection."

Terry's definition of love:

Love for me, is when we are attracted to both the inside and the outside of a person. Lust has already been satisfied and now there is a deeper feeling. We stop looking at someone with the naked eye and now can view their soul. We begin to look at them with our heart...

Chapter 5

So here we are engaged and her week couldn't get any better. She had been waiting for a call from the Police Academy and it came. My baby was going to be police officer. It was the year 2000, when my soon to be wife, went to the Police Academy. She attended the academy during the week and came home on the weekends. I missed her so much but I knew this was for her future.... our future. She came home amped up about all she had learned and talked about how once she became a police officer, she was going straight to the top. As her man and her number one cheerleader, I was right there with her.

I remember her graduation like it was yesterday. I couldn't have been more proud. I stood there with flowers for my queen, with her daughter by my side. I watched as she spoke to other graduates, mostly men. I didn't allow that to make me think any less of my wife to be. I knew the police field was filled with men but she was engaged to me so I had no worries. She wore her ring proud at graduation and I was even more proud that I had given it to her.

Once she was back at home full time, her behavior began to change. She wanted to move, this place wasn't good enough. She wasn't happy. When I asked her why, she never had an answer. She began to talk more about money and how we needed more of it. As my queen, I was with her 100% and with her for the paper chase, as long as we did it together. I tried to be intimate with her but she was always tired. She was a new cop so it was a new kind of stress and strain on her so I didn't pay that much attention. She was still the apple of my eye even if I wasn't getting to her sweet spot as much as I would have liked.

She had been a cop for a short time and then I got a phone call from one of her closest friends.

"Terry, I need to talk to you." I said,

"Okay, so talk." She did the dramatic sigh.

"I know you are a good guy and you have always been a good guy and she's dumb for what she is doing and I just can't..." I cut off her theatrics and asked,

"Dumb for what? What are you talking about?" She sighed again.

"Terry, she is cheating on you with someone from the Academy…. I thought you had the right to know!" I swallowed hard.

"Naw, not my baby." I was in complete denial that the love of my life that wore my ring, and was going to be my wife could cheat on me. She laughed a little bit.

"Terry, are you kidding me? You haven't noticed she has been M.I.A. a bit? She is not working overtime she is working him overtime. She told me she hasn't even been giving you any. It is all going to him." I felt my face flush at this girl knowing our in-house business. As I am talking to this girl, she walks in. I say,

"Well look, I appreciate you calling and giving me that information. I will look into it, but right now my baby just walked in the house, I have to go." I hung up the phone and looked at her. She smiled at me and kissed me. No way was she cheating on me. I pulled on her clothes and she said,

"I'm tired." I said,

"I don't care I'm getting some tonight." She smiled at me and went and showered. When she came out the shower I was waiting for her. I got up in her guts so far that if she even thought about cheating she would stop. I laid it down to make her remember why she even said yes to begin with. I rolled off her satisfied that I had done my job. She laid under me and I fell off to sleep. The next day her friend called me back.

"Terry, she said she had to have sex with you last night but she didn't want to because she had just had sex with him. I am telling you Terry she is playing you and you don't deserve it." I was tired of her jealous friend lying on her.

"Look why would you lie on my baby like that?" She sighed.

"Yo put your phone on mute and don't say shit. Watch this." She called my baby on three way and got her to repeat the story of how she was sexing her coworker and how good it was. Her friend asked,

"What about Terry?" She replied,

"What about him? We ain't married yet. That's my man but I am just having a little fun before I get married." Her friend laughed,

"Girl I hear you! Well you know I got your back, don't you?" She laughed,

"I know you do, that's why I love you…let me get going I will call you later." She hung up and I sat there, just listening. The friend said,

"See Terry I told you. You need to leave her alone…There are real women out here that wouldn't take you for granted like she is doing. What you doing tonight?" I was dejected and said,

"Nothing…"She said,

"Why don't you come see me?" I said,

"Huh?" She laughed,

"You heard me. I said why don't you come see me tonight?"

I took down her address and looked at it. We had agreed on a time and everything. I slowly ripped her address into pieces and flushed it down the toilet. I couldn't do the one I loved that way…. and, I don't know how she could do me, the one she claimed to love that way…

I began to call her phone like crazy. She didn't answer. I left 3 messages. The first one I was going off; the next one I had calmed down but by the third message I was going off again. I threatened to cut up and bleach all her clothes. I know people will judge me but I was not raised to treat women with nothing less than respect. I wanted to thrash her, but I wouldn't because I am not and never will be a woman beater. She called her friend and told her she was scared to go home. I kept calling until she finally answered. When she came in the door she started with the tears. I couldn't even be mad. I immediately dropped my attitude and apologized to her. Here she was cheating on me and I was apologizing to her. I told her we could work it out. I loved her. She was human and had made a mistake, so I forgave her…biggest mistake of my life.

ISSUE #3 BETRAYAL

The definition of betrayal is: "The breaking or violation of trust, or confidence that produces moral and psychological conflict within a relationship amongst individuals.

Terry's definition of betrayal:

The best term I can come up with is "messed up." When someone has done us so dirty and we know we don't deserve it, all trust goes out of the window. It's a Mother-sucker is what it is. It hurts like hell. People don't know the damage they can do when they do us wrong like this. Betrayal can change our whole outlook on life. It changes us and shapes us as a person. Our innocence is lost and now we know what true hurt feels like…

Chapter 6

We decided to work it out and stay together. She was still semi cold but a little warm. One day I came home from work and she was sitting on the bed crying. I ran to her got on my knees and asked,

"What's wrong?" She replied,

"You! This! My daughter's father wants me back! He said I am his soulmate and I want to go." I looked at her with tears developing in my eyes.

"After all we been through you want to throw it all in and go back to him?" She cried,

"I never wanted this to happen but I deserve to give him another chance." I sighed,

"Well I love you enough to let you go. I will pack my stuff and leave." I left. I decided enough was enough.

She didn't try to stop me. I found myself calling her. Here she had done me dirty and I was begging her to take me back. After a few weeks of pleading, she decided she missed me and wanted to be back with me. When I arrived back in our home she tried to talk about it. I shh'd her with a kiss to her lips. We didn't need to rehash the past. I was home where I was going to stay…or so I thought…

I was now 26 and she was 23. It was 2002 and we decided to go on our first vacation together. We went on a cruise to the Bahamas. I remember standing on the deck of the cruise watching her in the moonlight. Life couldn't get any better for me…

ISSUE #4 QUICK FORGIVENESS

The definition of forgiveness is: "The action or process of forgiving or being forgiven."

Terry's definition of forgiveness:

I believe in forgiveness. I believe we must forgive someone to be able to move on and continue to love that person. If we don't practice forgiveness, the pain will eat us up inside. I believe in forgiving and forgetting. We can't move on if we are dwelling on the past. So, I forgive people, this doesn't mean I am going to play the fool though. I can forgive, forget, and move on…but alone…

PART 3

MARITAL BLISS…

The definition of bliss is: "Perfect happiness; great joy."

Terry's definition of Marital Bliss:

Marital Bliss for me was the happiest day of my life next to my son being born. I took my marriage seriously, why? Because it was what I wanted. I grew up with 2 married parents. They may have fussed and fought a little, but that was just growing pains. They stuck it out and are still married to this day. My Father is my hero. I wanted to be just like him, so being married and staying married was my goal. I believed in the sanctity of marriage. I was dedicated to one woman and one woman only. I thought that same courtesy would have been extended to me by my wife…but it wasn't….

Chapter 7

It was now the year 2003 and everything was good between she and I. We moved to a bigger place on Derby in East Orange. We were back in love like we were in the beginning of our relationship. We planned to have a baby. She was pregnant and I was the happiest man on earth. She convinced me we should move again, new beginnings. I agreed to that, as long as she agreed to marry me now. I wanted my family to have my last name. It was 2004 and we decided upon a small wedding with family and friends.

After the wedding was over and my son was born, I figured she would really want to be grounded, and stay home with the baby, but she wanted just the opposite. She had barely recovered from having my son before she hit the streets again. I was the at home, Mr. Mom and she was the Roadrunner in the streets. The rumors began to fly starting with her messing with a Sergeant from her job, this guy and that guy but it hurt so much that I never even bothered to question her about it. We were Christians above all else so I prayed. I prayed that I didn't kill her and prayed for God to change her mind and bring her back to me. She had it all but was out in the streets behaving like she was a single woman. I never let her know that I had heard anything about her escapades. I gladly watched the kids when she wanted to go out and gave her my love when she wanted it, which wasn't very often. I loved being a father and I occupied my mind by concentrating on the kids....

ISSUE #5 PRIORITIES

The definition of priorities is: "A thing that is regarded as more important than another."

Terry's definition of priorities:

Before we have children with anyone, we should make sure that our priorities line up. For me, the children were my first priority, especially when in competition with hanging out with my friends or partying. I never forced anything on anyone, marriage and kids was something that I believed we both wanted. It is a messed up feeling when your spouse chooses fun and good times over home but it happens...

Chapter 8

So here it was now 2005. She once again began to act oddly and I, being in denial, couldn't figure out why. She wanted to move saying we needed a new place, I was down with it. Anything to keep my baby happy. We decided to buy a house in Newark on Noll Street. Our son was turning 1. She went from Nine West to Louboutin's. She began to change the way she dressed and how she spent money. She ran out and got her first BMW. I was happy for my wife and excited she could get the things she liked.

After we moved into our new home, a movie theater opened in East Orange and she signed up to work overtime there. It was easy money. A police presence always helped people to reevaluate any trouble they may have wanted to cause. My wife worked and I could spend time with our children. We were a team so we worked together as one.

We were coined the Huxtables. We had this loving family and all our friends and family were welcomed at any time. We would throw big cookouts at the house. There was plenty of food, drinks and fun. I invited all my friends over and she did the same. She also invited many of her coworkers over. Little did I know, some of them were the men she cheated on me with. Here I was, welcoming her sex partners into my home.

Not long after, I noticed the coldness again that she had exhibited when she cheated on me previously. I didn't want to believe it. We had gotten past that challenge, so I assumed that the stress and demands of being a cop had her mind elsewhere. I didn't press her for sex. I loved and treated her the best way I knew how. I trusted her, why else did I marry her?

One day my phone rang and it was my cousin.

"Yo T, I seen your broad in her car with a dude in the passenger seat. She's cheating on you." My head spun, face flushed. She couldn't be doing this again, could she? I called her,

"Hey, who is in the car with you?"

She replied, "Nobody. I just dropped off my coworker. His car is in the shop. I am driving home now. Why did you ask me that?" I sighed,

"No reason baby. I'll see you when you get here." I felt horrible for even thinking for a moment, that my woman could possibly be unfaithful again. We had moved on from her previous infidelity and we didn't talk about the past. We both lived in the present and looked forward to our future.

I called my cousin back and informed him that he must have been mistaken and could not have seen what he thought he saw. My cousin replied,

"Yeah all right," and hung up.

Weeks turned into months and my cousin called me again.

"Yo, I just saw this bitch. Same dude, same shit. They are messing around cousin. I seen them kissing at the light. I followed her and they were making out in the car. Do you want me to get out and handle this?" Embarrassed I said,

"Naw, it's cool cousin I got it." He spoke angrily.

"Yo you sure? I will beat both they asses out here. I don't care nothing about that cop shit." I laughed,

"Naw, it's cool. Don't worry about it. Thanks for letting me know though." I was on fire. She blatantly lied to me about this dude. When she said he was her coworker, I thought he was a police officer, but I found out later he just worked at the movie theater. Now there is nothing wrong with a hardworking man, but he cleaned the theater! I felt like, here I was making strides and moving up in my career and she was messing with the help.

When she came home I was yelling from the time she walked in the door. The tears fell. I calmed down, and apologized once again, even though I wasn't the one who was wrong. I asked her to forgive me for yelling and asked her to stay. She said she had to go, she wasn't happy and this wasn't for her. I asked again, 'What are you not happy with?' She could never answer that question. What she did was gather

her things and move out. She left the kids with me and moved out I guess to find herself…

ISSUE #6 ABANDONMENT

The definition of abandonment is: "The action or fact of abandoning or being abandoned."

Terry's definition of Abandonment

Abandonment is just getting up and leaving. The person just has no more fight in them. They don't want to try to make it work. It is often easier to run than to face our problems. It is a cruel way to treat someone you say you love. It left me feeling empty inside and as a man I felt even worse because there was no one I could confide in. It isn't okay for a man to talk to his buddies about being sad. My boys wanted to make sure I was good, so of course I could show no sign of weakness...but being abandoned felt like the air had just left my body. I didn't want to go on, but I knew I had to. Being left is a horrible feeling....

PART 4

THE HONEYMOON IS OVER

The definition of the honey moon is over is: "The initial harmonious period in a new relationship has ended.'

Terry's definition of The Honeymoon is Over:

I know. Life is busy and things get in the way. Your marriage goes from being fun, to being a chore. It becomes routine, but anything worth having, is worth working for. Nothing comes easy, not even marriage. The love is still there during this time, but it is just different. All changes don't have to be bad…

Chapter 9

After she moved out I stayed in the house. While I was there paying bills, she decided to put the house up for sale. Here I was separated, a single father of 2, not dating, and not seeing anyone. All I did was work and raise my kids. She and I spoke on the phone and I'd ask her to come home, but she always declined. I prayed to God to save my marriage…be careful what you pray for. She ended up coming back home. The problem was she had already sold our home. She came to me crying and said that she had changed her mind and didn't want to sell it. Now she wanted to stay. I contacted a lawyer and the potential buyer took us to court. We had to pay him $2,400.00 to keep our house.

She was back full time. We were back in love and got to keep our house. About a year later she wanted to sell the house again and move to Lebanon, NJ. I obliged. My love for my wife was deeper than anything I had ever experienced. When she looked at me, I wanted to be the only man she had eyes for. Once we got to Lebanon it didn't take long before she was up to her old tricks again. The 'I am not happy' speech became a part of her genetic makeup. The cold shoulder, treating me badly, I could no longer take it. I decided this time I was going to move. I was going to play, I was going to do me!

I left, found an apartment in Irvington but I never got around to playing. I was a married man and I could not bring myself to betray my wedding vows. So, I worked, worked and worked some more. She moved out of our place in Lebanon and moved in with her girlfriend.

I could tell from her routine that she had found a new dude. I didn't even investigate. I went to work and I came home. I would get my kids and do my best to be a good father and that was all. 6 months went by, and she started calling me, asking me how I was, and did I miss her? She told me that she missed me. I had it bad for my wife. I allowed her to come live with me in Irvington. I guess the grass on the new dudes' side wasn't any greener than the grass on my side. Once she came home, I didn't ask who she had been with, I never discussed who, where, when, what or why. I was just happy that we were together again. The entire time she was out "finding herself" I sat at home…waiting…

ISSUE #7 FAITHFHUL TO THE UNFAITHFUL

The definition of faithful is: "Loyal, constant, firm in adherence to whatever one owes allegiance."

The definition of unfaithful is the opposite.

Terry's definition of faithful to the unfaithful:

This subject causes great sadness in me. Being unfaithful to a loving mate is totally disrespectful and uncalled for. Infidelity causes deep hurt, sadness and anger in the innocent mate. In my case, I felt I was giving so much of myself and not only was I not receiving anything back, she was giving what was mine to someone else.

Chapter 10

For the next several years, we were chugging right along, doing well. The year was 2008 and Social Media was now the popular way to connect with old friends and family. Facebook was the new forum and both she and I had a Facebook page. This simply proved to be another way for her to establish relationships with other men. She stayed on social media.

I wasn't as tech savvy, and wasn't familiar with all of the intricate workings of Facebook.

One day I was sitting at the computer, on Facebook. I got up and left my page open. She jumped on the computer and shortly after started screaming my name,

"TERRY WHAT ARE ALL THESE INBOXES!" I had no idea what an 'inbox' was. I came back to the computer and said,

"What are you talking about?"

She clicked on my inbox and I had a bunch of messages from girls. Some had naked pictures, some said I know you married but forget your wife, I want to give you some, and others were just people I knew from around the way but my wife was on fire. She knew I had never read them because the messages hadn't been opened. She looked at me with jealousy in her eyes. I smiled inside, thinking, 'My wife does love me. She is jealous…' Little did I know, she merely wanted to have her cake and eat it too. Not much time passed before she started again with the same old, "I'm not happy" speech.

She said she had to move out. I loved her enough to let her go. I treated her like a butterfly…if she returned to me, we were meant to be together. She got an apartment in Carteret and I stayed in Irvington. I had to give her some space and hoped that this might ultimately draw us closer. I was chasing her. I loved my wife. I told her we should date again and we did. We went out on dates and then she would go home to her house and I went home to mine. She invited me over and cooked for me. We came together for family night but at the end of the day, we always went our separate ways. When my lease was up, she suggested I come back home with her and the children and be a full-time family again. I obliged and moved to Carteret.

Everything was getting back to normal, just the way it should be. We were a couple again, a married couple. We had 2 beautiful kids. We traveled together, wore matching colors, and took family pictures for the holidays. We were like the Huxtables. We just had so much fun. Our sex life was extremely healthy. She seemed to be happy, and never gave me the cold shoulder. I was in bliss.

One day in 2011 she came home and announced we needed to move again. I swallowed hard. This was the behavior that always started the cycle. I didn't want to believe that once again, I was competing with some other dude for my wife's attention and affection. I reasoned, 'Maybe she was tired of where we were and really did just want to move to a different location.' So, we moved to Mount Olive. We rented a house. We weren't in the house a week before she began giving me the cold shoulder again. Mind you, she was my best friend while I was spending my money, preparing for and moving into this new home. It was as if as soon as the fresh paint was dry, she came at me with the, "I'm not happy" speech again.

She began to talk on the phone in hushed tones. I'd see her pull up outside and stay in the car for an hour or sometimes two. Her phone was attached to her hip. She never left it around. I knew that I had been replaced with someone new, the day she called me Terry. I was no longer "baby," "babe" or "bae." I ignored all these signs again, because I loved my wife and wanted my marriage to survive. No matter what anyone else thought about my wife, I thought she was dope. I wanted her, and she wanted to separate. I didn't want to see her unhappy, so I agreed. Once the lease was up, I moved into my own apartment and she moved in with her girlfriend.

ISSUE #8 BLINDED

The definition of blinded is: "something that causes (someone) to be unable to see."

Terry's definition of blinded:

Thinking I had the total package in a wife; beauty, brains, the bomb sex…. all of the qualities a man wants his wife to have. I couldn't see who she really was, because I believed this was my best friend. We were silly together, we would dream together, we had built a life together. …I don't know how long I had my blinders on, but they are off now…I can see.

PART 5

CHANGES

The definition of changes is: "To make or become different."

Terry's definition of change:

Change is sometimes good and sometimes bad. As far as my marriage was concerned, I wanted it to change for the better but unfortunately, it changed for the worse. We had a routine, a normal life, or so I thought, but for my wife, that just wasn't enough....

Chapter 11

So it was 2012 and we were officially separated. We co parented but I wanted more. I wanted my wife back. My apartment and her girlfriend's apartment were close to one another. I called her and if I talked about anything other than the kids, she'd say she had to go. I asked her did she miss me and she said no. Whoever this guy was, must have blown her mind. I was chasing my wife and my wife was chasing another man. She was very cold to me and treated me as if I was the dirt under her feet, as though we had never loved each another. . I wore my ring while she took hers off. I was heartbroken.

My phone was blowing up with calls from my family, her family, my friends, her friends…they were all checking on me to make sure I was okay. This made me think they may have known something I didn't know. Whatever it was, I didn't want to know. I was stressed out and my kids were stressed out. They were old enough to ask questions and I had no answers.

Then one day it changed. She called and said the kids wanted her to cook dinner. I said,

"Ok." She said,

"I want to cook at your house, is that okay?" I smiled inside.

"Yeah, that is fine." When I got home that day, she had cooked all my favorite foods. We sat down to the table together like a family and ate. She told me she wanted to get more comfortable before she cleaned up after dinner. She went into my bedroom and put on one of my t shirts and just her panties. I swallowed hard, looking at her and seeing how good she looked to me. I was tired of being a doormat, so I willed my little head to stay down. After she cleaned the kitchen, she made sure the kids were okay and in bed, and then got dressed and left. I didn't stop her.

A few days later she asked me to meet her for dinner. I agreed. We sat down at the Chart House and chatted about nothing, mostly BS. We talked about the kids and then she finally admitted,

"I miss my husband." I didn't have anything to say. She said,

"Well does my husband miss me?" I told her,

"You know I miss you and I love you but you keep doing the same thing over and over. I don't deserve to be treated like that." She agreed,

"You are right! I love you Terry. I won't ever betray you again! Let's make it work again…I want another baby." Having a baby, was music to my ears. I wanted another one. We left the Chart House and couldn't get home fast enough. We made love from the night to the morning. I loved her and I was now back in her good graces. I let her move back in to our home.

She wanted a new home so we went house hunting. We were looking for the perfect place, which was hard to find so we decided to get a house built from the ground up. We found a location, broke ground and the contractor began building our new house.

ISSUE #9 STUPIDITY

The definition of stupidity is: "Behavior that shows a lack of good sense or judgment."

Terry's definition of Stupidity

They say stupid is, as stupid does. My intelligence and common sense were evident but my actions showed something completely different. I acted like I was insane. I was practicing insanity. I did the same things over and over again, expecting a different outcome. I felt that if I showed and expressed more love for her, or practiced a little more patience with her or gave more of myself, this time our marriage would last, this time it would be different…but it never was...

Chapter 12

It was now the year 2013 and I was in love. I encouraged her to have the baby she said she wanted but she told me she had to wait a few months until she built up some time at work. I had fun just trying to get her pregnant. We moved into our house, which we had built from the ground up and for the first time the look on my wife's face read happy. I was happy I was making her happy.

We picked out all new furniture. Raymour & Flanigan. Only the best for the love of my life. We bought clothing in matching colors and took family pictures. Now, Instagram was popping and we both had an Instagram page. We posted each other's pictures constantly, showing the world our love for each other. I placed emoji's with heart eyes on her page and she blew kisses on mine. Our names matched and she was the Mrs. to my Mr. Everything was going well.

We planned and took vacation trips, trips with couples, and family trips. We were stuck like glue. She talked about how ALL her friends were whores and how she would never be like them, meanwhile she was the ring leader. Along with social media came the bull crap.

I am not a conceited dude, but I am not an ugly dude by any stretch of the imagination. I've heard it said that a persons' looks on the outside are enhanced by the person they are on the inside and I must say, I am pretty awesome. I'm polite, complimentary and view black women as the queens that they are. Me just being the man I am, caused my Direct Messages on Instagram to blow up. But I was not interested in anyone hitting me up on DM. I loved my wife. She went onto my Instagram page and saw messages to me from these women and hit block on all of them. She questioned me constantly about who this was and who that girl was, so to keep the peace and because social media meant nothing to me, I deleted and blocked them all. I wasn't the jealous type, so I enjoyed men lusting over my wife. I knew who she came home to.

We had a good two year run but the ultimate bullshit came in December of 2015. Someone mentioned to me that they saw my wife out with some dude. I thought, 'Here we go again' but she hadn't given me her now infamous "I'm not happy" speech and her movements and routine hadn't changed. At this point, I knew some people just liked to hate on black love, so I chalked it up to that and ignored this first warning. . My mother was having a big birthday celebration and we all went as a family. We were happy, we took pictures, shared kisses and all that until the party was almost over and then she snapped. She tried to start an argument with me in front of my cousins and then she left. I didn't know this was a set up to go see her new dude. I just let her go and let her calm down. We drove separately to the party so it was easy for her to just leave. When we both reached home that night, she pretended to have an attitude and I allowed her to have it. I had been drinking at the party and had a nice buzz and was not in the mood for her games.

Christmas was a week or two away. She continued to pretend to have an attitude with me and I was so fed up that at this point, I just let her have one. . I asked her what she wanted for Christmas and she told me she didn't want anything. So, I gave her what I thought all females loved to get, money. I went to her bank account and dropped a stack in there to buy herself what she wanted. This wasn't good enough. This was just the excuse she needed to give me the "I'm not happy" speech. I was finally tired. I told her to pack her stuff and leave and that this time was going to be the last time.

She started with the tears, but I wasn't moved. She told me she didn't want to see me with anyone else and that it would hurt her to see me with someone else. I just let her talk. She was leaving me, it wasn't like I was leaving her. I was fed up with her and her antics at this point. I didn't even see her the same way anymore. Looking at her, all I saw was all of those different men from the past. For the first time, I looked at my wife for the harlot she was. My main priority at this point was my son.

Our daughter was grown and off at college and had a boyfriend. At first my ex wasn't crazy about the boy, but then all of a sudden she started doing things for him. She paid his dentists' bill and helped him with some other things. I wondered why she suddenly loved our daughter's boyfriend. That comes later.

She didn't leave right away, and weeks and weeks went by and we just walked around like the other didn't exist. She then did what I felt was the utmost disrespectful shit. She talked on the phone with dudes and with her friends about dudes. She did this purposefully within earshot of me and didn't care. One day, I was fed up and lost my temper. . She was upstairs in the bedroom talking about some dude and I yelled up,

"You are not going to continue to disrespect me in my house! If you want to talk to niggas or about them take that shit outside." I was so angry and yelling so loud I made myself nervous. I am usually able to always keep a cool head, but she was trying my patience. She took her phone outside to her car. We still slept in the same bed, back to back. I didn't try to touch her and she didn't try to touch me.

My birthday was February 13 and she sent me a text message saying happy birthday and that was it. A week later my boys took me out and she called me. She wanted to have all these dudes and me too and that wasn't going to happen anymore. She was on her bipolar ish. She tells me again,

"I'm sorry I love you, I want my husband." I didn't melt at the sound of her voice, and told her,

"You have just been too disrespectful. It's over. I just want you to get your stuff and go." I hung up. I sighed. She was still my wife, I still loved her…. or so I thought....

When I got home, she insisted on talking to me and trying to work it out. I allowed myself to listen to her. I fell for it. We took out our calendars and planned family vacations. We both put our requests for vacation days in at work and we were cordial. A few short weeks later she claimed she had made a mistake. She still wasn't happy and she wanted out of this marriage. I was over her. I couldn't and wouldn't live like this. I asked her when she was leaving. I left to get away from her.

A week later it was her birthday, love was still blinding me and I went to Short Hills Mall and bought her a pair of $1,000 Versace shoes. She barely said thank you, tried them on and then said they were too tight and she needed to get dressed because she and her friends were hitting the town for her birthday. She claimed they were heading to Tao in the city and she knew she would probably be drunk, so she was staying at her friend's house that night. I didn't care at this point.

Well, the first thing most people do when they are out is post pictures on "The gram." Mind you, her friends and I were all friends, so I was scrolling my time line and all her friends were wishing her a happy birthday. But the pictures coming up appeared to be of her in a hotel room. I guess Tao had changed. I noticed every pic that she posted, a dude with a familiar name that I recognized, was liking each picture. I remembered him communicating with her a lot on her page so I clicked on his public page and lo and behold he had a picture up with the same hotel background saying he was out of town. I was livid. This woman thought I was dumb. She told me a blatant lie about being out with her girls and she was with this dude. It was cool though. I was going to show her.

We were still living together in the same house which made it very hard to be cordial. When I came in from work after her weekend away she was luxuriating in our hot tub soaking in the bath. I came in the bathroom to get in the shower and just looked at her in disgust. Here she was slutting her body out all weekend and just laying back with no worries. I got in the shower and we argued back and forth. I had never called her out of her name but she was everything but a child of God on that day. She had a smart mouth and told me she'd do what she wanted to do and that made my temper rise. I felt like I could reach out and touch her and not in a loving way but my son began to cry so I decided to leave. I hugged my son to calm him down, while I flipped her off behind my sons back. I left and drove around aimlessly. I could not believe it had come to this. All the times she had cheated and this was going to be the last.

I stayed away for a few days and she didn't call me nor did I call her. She finally sent a text message to me, saying she was moving out. She moved while I was at work. I came back to our home and she was gone and it was like a breath of fresh air had blown through. I haven't fronted throughout this whole book and I won't do it now. I was sick. I couldn't eat, I couldn't sleep. My parents had been married for about 40 years and I had barely made it to 10. I had good friends, both male and female, who had my back and who had picked me up and brushed me off at one of the lowest times of my life. They let me know my worth and told me it was her loss. . I had never prayed so much as I did during this time and I was one who prayed constantly. One day I woke up and it was as if a weight had been lifted from my chest. The power of God is real. No matter how dark your situation is, prayer will change things. God placed the right people around me and they really helped me to get past my heartbreak, but even now, it wasn't over.

I now had to prepare my kids for a divorce, and prepare myself to be single at 40. I had to come to grips with the fact that my so called happily ever after, was never going to be. One of the down sides of being a popular couple is that word comes back faster than a fire can spread. Some people love to share bad news. I was receiving calls left and right about different ones' seeing her and this dude hugged up in the Fox Trap, a local bar in Irvington and hugged up in The Atmosphere, a local bar in Newark. I was disgusted that she didn't even respect me, the marriage or her children enough to hang out in another part of town. I remember when we were together, she turned her nose up at the Fox Trap like she was better than that. She said she would die before she went into Atmosphere and this had become her second home. Me, I had no desire to hang out like that and planned to just chill and be a better father.

As if things, couldn't get any worse my cousin called me a few weeks later going off He was screaming into the phone,

"F that B and move out of that house." I asked,

"Why?" and he said,

"Do you know that B is 4 months pregnant by that dude?" My heart dropped. We had just spoken of having another baby together a few months ago, and now she was having another baby but with this new dude. At that point I didn't even know how "new" he was. He could have been with her while we were married, who knew? I just got hot around the collar knowing she had been lying next to me, pregnant by another man. Talk about trifling. There was nothing else I could ever say to her again.

She texted things to me about our son, and I ignored them. My son was old enough to communicate with her directly and we didn't ever have to speak again. I called a few of close friends to vent about this whole situation. Folks around town were saying this dude had put pictures of ultrasounds up on social media. By this time, I was off of social media and I didn't care. All of that was her problem. I stayed strong, and carried on.

About two weeks later that same cousin called me again and said, "Ain't God good?" I agreed,

"Yeah God is great." He said,

"I am trying to tell you! That B had a miscarriage." I laughed a bit,

"Come on Cuz, don't bring God into that." He laughed,

"Man F#ck that B#tch! I am happy for her." I didn't know how to feel. I am not hateful, spiteful or any of those negative things so I did what I knew how to do, I prayed for her. I believed in my heart of hearts, that I would never take this girl back, and I had no ill feelings towards her. I wished her all the best. I gave her ample opportunities to treat me like crap, but I didn't blame anyone but myself and love.

Chapter 13

April 26th, 2016 my divorce was final. I never thought I'd see this day. During the time I was going through the pain of this break-up, I met a friend. I am no hypocrite, she was just a friend. I knew her from my past and she reached out to me when she heard what was going through. I attribute getting through that rough patch to her. She picked me up from the dirt and basically nursed me back to health. She was my diary and my therapist and I could tell her everything. She didn't judge me or call me weak. She was a friend to me, she encouraged me and kept me grounded. I appreciated her but even after all that I still thought of my wife. When I moved past the anger, I realized I didn't hate her anymore and this became a separation point in my relationship between myself and my friend.

We finally took our friendship to the next level which sometimes is not a good idea because sex confuses things. We traveled to Canada together and the old cliché "It wasn't her, it was me" was true. I couldn't enjoy being with her, my mind was somewhere else. She was devastated. She felt like there was something wrong with her, but there wasn't anything wrong with her. . She is beautiful, smart and faithful but I just wasn't ready. She felt like I was hiding my relationship with her, while my ex was out flaunting her new love to the world.

I finally introduced her to my children and allowed her to come into the home that I had shared with my wife. My son was shy at first but came around a little bit. My daughter instantly liked her and was happy for me.

My son was loyal to me and whenever he came home from his mother's house he said,

"You are my only father!" I'd reply,

"Yes, I am your only father." Situations like this are confusing for kids….hell it's confusing for adults. The relationship with my friend was moving way too fast, as the ink wasn't even dry on my divorce papers. The divorce had been granted and I wasn't sure that it was what I really wanted.

Day by day I began to notice more and more of my friend's things were ending up in my closet. I told her it was too much and too fast for me. She looked at me as though she knew something bad was coming.

July 2, 2016 my ex-wife began texting me and told me that she missed me, she needed help and she wanted me back. I couldn't lie, I missed her and wanted her back too. I just wanted her to do right, be faithful and be a good wife. She asked me to meet her somewhere so I did.

We met up at our favorite steakhouse. When we saw one another, she looked me in my eyes and I looked in hers. All the hate was gone from my heart. I hugged her and kissed her on the cheek. Once we sat down she began crying. I just let her cry because I was no longer moved by her tears. She said she missed her family and wanted to end her life. I immediately softened. We talked about the hateful things we had said to one another in the past and apologized to each other. Leaving the restaurant, she said she knew what she wanted and it was to be back with her family.

I began to distance myself from my friend and she immediately sensed it. My ex-wife made sure she hit me up every other day, reminding me of what we had talked about and what she wanted. I told my friend I needed time to think and had to fall back. She came over to the house to get her things and asked me why, but I couldn't answer her. We exchanged words, but I had to follow my heart. I couldn't blame her for being hurt. I had just done to her what my ex-wife had done to me.

After that day, my wife and I began to semi date again. She came back to the house we shared and said,

"I can never sleep in that room, on that bed that you and your 'friend' slept on or even walk on that carpet." What did I do? I tore the carpet up, painted and bought a brand-new bedroom set. I did all of that for my **ex-wife**. When she and I were 100 percent back together and she had moved back in, we planned a family vacation to Vegas. Me, her and the kids. Her first week home, we had sex but in my heart, I was still skeptical. I could actually have sex with my ex-wife with no problems, but I felt I still couldn't trust her. She reassured me that I could trust her. She was with me 110 percent.

We went to Vegas and it was perfect. I rented a boat and we went out sailing and life was back to how it should be. We looked at properties in Vegas and talked about transferring out there to live. We played the perfect family. We got back to New Jersey and I took her to my family's cook out. She didn't really get a warm welcome, but she didn't get disrespected either. The family just didn't deal with her, but I didn't care. It was my life and this was how I wanted to live it.

My brother and I, the one whom I am closest to, fell out a bit. He didn't like it. He said,

"She is out here embarrassing you and has you looking like a clown and you are not a clown! She is." We exchanged words back and forth but it was what I wanted. The funny thing is, everything he was saying, I felt too but I hoped our love was stronger than my doubt.

My older sister and parents said they were with me as long as I was happy. I am close to my other sister as well, but she wasn't feeling it. She was on the same wavelength as my brother. She didn't speak to me at the cookout but because she really is not like that, the next day she called me and apologized. She just didn't appreciate how my ex-wife treated me and disrespected me by carrying on with these negroes in the streets. It may have been different if the whole hood didn't know, but everyone knew and my sister was upset. We made up quickly because that's my baby and she and I, we don't beef ever.

My cousin got married. He had a big beautiful wedding with the whole hood there and I took my wife. We danced, we laughed…we talked about getting married again. After the wedding, she was back to her old ways. I felt it in my soul. She hadn't changed one bit. One month had not gone by. . I had hurt my friend, someone who really cared about me, had problems with my siblings over her, remodeled the bedroom for her and she still wasn't done with those streets.

That next Thursday night, I called her. She said she was out with her friends and answered the phone like I was her homie, not her soon to be husband again. I waited up for her. When she got in the house I said,

"Listen, I have been reading my bible and talking to God and deep down in my heart I know you ain't right for me." The love wasn't strong enough, she was very selfish, she always talked about people, especially her so-called friends, she thinks she is better than everyone and this one I struggle with writing but it is the truth. We talked about having another baby, and she told me she didn't want another child with me because the genes in my family weren't right. I won't say anymore, but that was the nail in the coffin for me. I told her she needed mental help and I would pay for it.

She used me to get back in the house and I allowed it but it was time for me to make my exit.

I love myself more now. She is disrespectful, vindictive and a mental abuser. God was pulling me away and I wanted to follow God.

She actually agreed that we shouldn't be together. She said she tried it, but it just wasn't working for her. We went back and forth with each other. She told me about myself and I told her about herself. She had the nerve to say I turned the kids against her. I have never spoken a bad word to the children about their mother. They know I was there for them when she wasn't. I listened to them when she didn't. That night she moved into my son's room. Laying in my room alone, looking at all I had changed for her and thinking about all I had done for her, I shed a few tears but I slept well that night.

The next day she had a talk with the kids. My daughter was tired of the back and forth but my son didn't care much about us being a part. My daughter told me she was happy because I deserved to be happy. We put the house up for sale. My daughter came to me and said she was happy it was going on the market because it was nothing but pain, bad memories and stress in this house. I felt so bad for my child. They didn't deserve to have those kinds of memories.

I initially planned to wait for the house to sell, and then go my way and she could go hers but that was a torture I wasn't going to live with. I found a place big enough for myself and my kids to come home to and that is that. It feels good coming home to my own place. No stress, no aggravation.

During all this, she called me, crying and said that she couldn't afford to put tires on her car. I told her to meet me at the dealership and I swiped my credit card. She was dating another dude and said,

"He can't even afford to buy me tires." This was no longer my concern. My concern was for my children who would be riding in that car, so I bought the tires. Sucker or no sucker, I did it and now it's done.

I am proud of myself, that I was able to move on and move strong. I feel very different now. I know many will judge me for the last time I let her come back home, but I needed that. I needed to see who she really was and that she wasn't for me and I wasn't for her.

I found my happy place. I had to learn that happiness comes from within. All the songs about love and fools were all about me. Everybody plays the fool sometimes, there are no exceptions to the rules. I loved her but I love me more. Looking back, I should have left her a long time ago but hey, I didn't. The funny thing about social media outlets is everyone wants to be social. I get calls, texts daily about what she is doing. The thing is, I really don't care. I wish her all the best in her life and her relationship. It was also said that her new "friend" was related to my daughter's boyfriend. Made more sense to me as to why she began to do so much for him, after not being able to stand him. There are rumors of kids on the way, again it could be rumors or it could be true, all I know is, it is not my concern. I am sharing my story because as a man, we don't talk about how we get played.

Mental abuse is serious business. It can be more serious than physical abuse because physical scars heal, mental scars take longer to heal and if you don't get help they can take over your life. Society talks freely about how we as men break women's hearts, but as men we seldom talk about our heartbreak. As a man's man I say this, she hurt me, she hurt me bad. I am not going to put up any brave front. I was hurt. The bravery comes from writing this book because men don't admit such things as these but I am.

I am telling you that your truth is your truth. You live it, walk in it, talk it, be it and own it. My truth is, I am a good person who got wrapped up in the wrong person. I tasted fruit from that poisonous tree but now I know better. Life is about learning from our mistakes, making improvements and doing better, and trust me, I am going to do my best to be the best Terry I know how to be. Peace…

EPILOGUE

Throughout this experience, I have encountered a number of people who shared things with me about my ex-wife. Nothing compares to one. This was a true woman of God, who told me about certain things that would take place in my life, and they happened. The first time, I ignored it, thinking it was a coincidence, but now I know that prophets are real.

She is someone I knew as a child. At this time, I had completely removed myself from social media, so she contacted my brother. When she called me by my God given government name I knew she was someone I knew from school. She continued to contact my brother and he finally called her back. He gave her my contact information and she called me.

She started the conversation with,

"How are you doing?" My response was,

"Fine." She was persistent and said,

"I know everything is not fine. I have been having dreams about you and your marriage." I was never close to her, so I surely wasn't going to pour out my heart and soul and let her know that she was right, everything wasn't fine. I just told her, no, everything was fine and she eventually back off a little and said,

"Ok."

From then on she called me daily, wanting to know how I was and my response was always,

"I'm still fine."

She revealed things to me about my marriage and ex-wife, that had not happened and were to come and they all came true. When she shared some things with me, I just had to tell her,

"I don't want to know."

The biggest thing she shared with me was regarding a dream she had. In this dream, I was in a park sitting on a bench. She was running in the park and joined me on the bench. I was busy writing and she said,

"Are you writing a book?" I replied that I was. The funny thing is, I had never shared with her that I was writing a book. I'd never even told her of my desire to write a book, for one. Once I confirmed to her that I was writing a book, she said she saw me traveling the world telling my story. My story wasn't an easy one to tell, but I told it. My story is my truth and how I perceived my life. I didn't write this story to degrade or belittle anyone. I wrote my story to share with the world my experience and what I learned from being married to the wrong person. The following are 10 life lessons that I live by daily, that have given my life direction and meaning. . I hope they help you just as they have helped me!

LIFE LESSON #1

1 Corinthians 13:11 "When I was a child, I spoke as a child, I understood as a child, I thought as a child: but when I became a man, I put away childish things.

This is the first lesson everyone needs to know when going from being a boy to man. I lusted after my wife instead of first loving my life. I thought with my little head instead of the big one. This can and will always get you into trouble. We must get to a certain place in life, where we look at people through God's eyes. It is so much more important to see the inner person, and not the outer. Someone can look so good to you on the outside, but their insides, who they are as a person may be ugly. This is a formula for disaster.

In order to know what to even look for in a wife, a man must first know the Word, to understand what he should look for in a wife. Once we understand God's plan and design it will become clearer who your wife is because God will reveal her to you. She might not be the prettiest woman by society's standards but she will be the most beautiful by God's standards. As you grow up and grow in your walk with your Creator, you will learn that only his standards matter, not societies. This is my story.

LIFE LESSON #2

Proverbs 3:5-6 "Trust in the LORD with all your heart and lean not on your own understanding; in all your ways submit to him, and he will make your path straight."

Trust must be earned not given. Because I knew this person for so long, I automatically trusted her. I didn't think twice about trusting her because I thought I already knew her. Knowing someone's name and where they live is not knowing them. Having sex with a person, is not knowing them. Talking everyday all day is not knowing them, if you are not asking thought provoking questions. Really knowing someone is knowing their innermost and deepest thoughts, concerns and dreams. I knew how she liked to have sex, I knew what she liked to eat, but I didn't know her. Had I gotten to know her, I would have recognized that the things she thought and did would never work for me in the long run.

To truly trust, we must get to know the person first to feel comfortable allowing them inside of our mind and heart. Getting to know someone first, doesn't mean knowing their outer appearance. It means getting to know not only their actions, but the thought behind their actions, their sub conscious. This is the part of the mind that controls a person's actions and feelings. Most people are not even fully aware of their sub conscious, but if we pay attention and give ourselves time to get to know them, we can get a sense of how they think, feel, what their priorities are, and who they love and hate.

LIFE LESSON #3

Matthew 6:14-15 "For if you forgive other people when they sin against you, your heavenly Father will also forgive you. But if you do not forgive others their sins, your Father will not forgive your sins."

"What goes around comes around," a saying that is similar to the concept of karma but as a Christian I don't believe in karma. I believe that God fights our battles for us and we need to let go and allow Him to so. The way we treat others is how others will treat us. We will always "reap what we sow." When we mistreat others, our time to be mistreated will certainly come. . When someone is doing right by us and do not reciprocate, watch out! We can't talk to nor treat people any kind of way, and not expect some sort of repercussion.

Betrayal is not easy to forgive. Some people think they can never forgive betrayal, but we should remember, God forgives us as we forgive others and with God's help, we can do anything. When we take our lives into our own hands, it is a recipe for disaster. We need God to help us.

One of the truest things ever said is "When we forgive, it is more for us, than the other person." If we don't forgive we will be walking around filled with hate and anger and they will be going about their lives, living free and happy. We must forgive for our own mental health and stability.

Once we let the anger go we can move on in our lives. You will feel no hate towards the person or situation and can move on with your life. Remember, our memories fade with time and as time passes, it becomes easier to forgive. The initial hurt and anger that we feel is temporary, keep in mind that "this too shall pass." The easiest way I can describe forgiveness is just to say, "Let it go!"

LIFE LESSON #4

Ephesians 5:22-33 "Wives, submit to your own husbands, as to the Lord. For the husband is the head of the wife even as Christ is the head of the church, his body, and is himself its Savior. Now as the church submits to Christ, so also wives should submit in everything to their husbands. Husbands, love your wives, as Christ loved the church and gave himself up for her, that he might sanctify her, having cleansed her by the washing of water with the word."

Marriage is a super dope thing, when it is with the right person. There may be a woman out here that's good to you and good for you but you overlook her because her breasts aren't big enough or her butt is not big enough or her skin is not light enough or her hair is not long enough, but she loves you for you. She's not on your radar because we want what society says looks good on our arm, instead of what God says looks good and what will actually make us happy. We must really look beyond the external at the heart of a person to see if they are a suitable mate for marriage. If they're honest and their heart is pure and filled with love for God first and then for you, they may be a keeper. If they are your biggest cheerleader and want to see you win, are supporting you, speaking to you with respect and treating you as the king you are, she is the one. Far too often, people marry for a persons' good looks and external appearance. Looks will fade, hair gets thin, skin gets wrinkles but the heart seldom changes.

I would love to get married again, but to the right person and to someone who is going to be my forever. Marriage must be taken seriously and any disagreements or problems should be kept between the two of you. When we marry, two become one and both parties must be on the same page and see eye to eye. Both husband and wife want to work to keep the marriage exciting and fresh. As men, we want to honor our wives and make her feel beautiful. Send her flowers, just because. Rub her feet when she's tired and continue to make her feel special just as you did in the beginning of your relationship. These are the reasons she married you in the first place, these are the things that will make her fall in love with you over and over again. But this is a two-way street, the things she did for you that made you love her, she must continue as well. If either of you detour from this course, your marriage may run into road blocks or even worse, a dead end.

I will use my first marriage as a stepping stone towards what I want and don't want for my future. I know I want someone who speaks to me with respect, is loyal and faithful and who loves me for who I am and not for what I can do for them or what they can get from me.

LIFE LESSON #5

1 Timothy 3:5 "For if someone does not know how to manage his own household, how will he care for God's church?"

When we become an adult, our priorities have to be in order. The latest handbag, the newest sneakers-none of that matters when you have grown folk's bills. Trying to keep up with the Joneses becomes old very quickly. There is a difference between being able to afford something that we buy and just buying something that we want. Buying something that we really cannot afford goes hand in hand with trying to be something that we're not and trying to keep up appearances. My priorities are always to make sure that my children's needs are met first. Once they've been taken care of and I see that I have a little extra, then I can splurge a little on myself sometimes. Of course, all the household bills must be taken care of. This of course would include the mortgage/rent, car note, car insurance, life insurance and other bills. If I am lagging behind on my bills, how can I treat myself to anything? My fridge and pantry has to be stocked and these are all things that aren't obvious or apparent to anyone outside of your household. What other people think doesn't matter, why spend money we don't have to show people up, that could care less about you? The illusion of doing better is just that, an illusion. We are all out here struggling and doing our best to make ends meet. God said if we can't manage our own household, how can we be in charge of his business? All of this goes hand in hand with who we decide to marry. If a couple is not on the same page financially, it is hard for anything else to go right. We always hear that one of the biggest problems in a marriage is money. I don't think it is the money itself, it is how the money is spent. If one wants to blow money fast on the latest fashion and the other wants to pay the mortgage, arguments will ensue. Couples must be on the same page with their priorities before anything else. The only person worth competing with is 'you' from the day before, improve on that person. What is the point in looking good on the outside when inwardly you are stressed out and worried about bills? Be yourself and live for yourself, not other people.

LIFE LESSON #6

Isaiah 49:15-16 "Can a woman forget her nursing child, that she should have no compassion on the son of her womb? Even these may forget, yet I will not forget you. Behold, I have engraved you on the palms of my hands; your walls are continually before me."

Being a parent is much more than a full-time job, it is a forever job. I will never stop being a parent, no matter what. When something or someone is important to us, we will never abandon, leave or forget about it or them. When we have children, family time is important and means a lot to them and should mean the world to us. Children need to know that they are loved, that their needs are important to their parents and that they matter. Children are smarter than most give them credit for. They recognize change and see when things are not as they should be. They realize when one parent is doing more than the other. These little ones, we say we love the most, should never feel or be abandoned. When children feel hurt or abandoned, their attitude may begin to change, their school work may suffer, they may begin acting out at school or they may become withdrawn and distant. Our job as parents, is to make sure our kids never feel anything but loved. My first and most important job will forever be that of a parent.

LIFE LESSON #7

1 Corinthians 7:10-11 "To the married I give this charge (not I, but the Lord): the wife should not separate from her husband (but if she does, she should remain unmarried or else be reconciled to her husband), and the husband should not divorce his wife."

Matthew 19:9 "I say to you that whoever divorces his wife, except on the grounds of sexual immorality, and marries another commits adultery."

Marriage should be a forever commitment. No one should be able to shake you from your marriage when you are truly one. Circumstances and situations may change but the marriage should remain constant. I took my marriage vows seriously. For better, for worse…for richer, for poorer…in sickness and in health. I thought that our love would last forever and I believe in being faithful to the end. Even in the face of unfaithfulness, I was faithful. Never lose sight of who you are even in the worst of circumstances. Never allow the bad behavior of others to cause you to act out of your character. . Getting a divorce was the last thing on my mind but I could not change the way my wife viewed our marriage, I could only change myself and the way I dealt with her. . I am a faithful man, I always have been and always will be. Be true to yourself first, be committed to your goals, stand by your morals and be loyal to your faith. I know what God said about divorce but sometimes it's inevitable, and he did make provisions for divorce as it relates to sexual immortality.

LIFE LESSON #7 part 2

1 Corinthians 7:15 "But if the husband or wife who isn't a believer insists on leaving, let them go. In such cases the Christian husband or wife* is no longer bound to the other, for God has called you* to live in peace."

If your spouse wants to leave, let them go. It is ok to try to work things out but you can't make someone stay with you when they want to leave, and don't beg anyone to stay. When we do that, they may still want to leave, but might stay out of pity. Nobody wants love with pity as its foundation. We want to be genuinely loved for who we are, that real, unbreakable bond that we dreamt about when we were young. If our mate decides to leave or breaks the marriage vow, we have to be willing to deal with our new reality, and be ready to move on and get strong.

LIFE LESSON #8

2 Corinthians 4:4 "In their case the god of this world has blinded the minds of the unbelievers, to keep them from seeing the light of the gospel of the glory of Christ, who is the image of God."

A person's actions and movement will show us all we need to see, when we are seeing with our eyes of discernment and not with our blinded eyes. The way my ex behaved and moved, I thought she wanted to be a family person but I saw what I wanted to see. She told me all the things I wanted to hear with her words but her actions told me what she really wanted and what was on her heart. She never spoke what was really on her heart. When arguments arose, I heard the truth but I just thought she was coming from a place of anger, and not a place of truth. Everything about her was a front or a disguise hiding who she really was. I learned that especially when social media became popular. We have to use what is known as our third eye when dealing with love and relationships. When the blinders are on, our third eye should be wide open. We have to pay close attention to the mood swings, the selfishness and the unappreciative spirit of a person. When we are giving our all and they still are not happy, their unhappiness has little to do with you and everything to do with something inside of them. . Often in a marriage, we try to solve a problem we are not even a part of. We try to make things right with a person who has a struggle within themselves. They have to address these things for themselves and we have to focus on what we can control, and that is ourselves.

LIFE LESSON #9

Hebrews 13:8 "Jesus Christ is the same yesterday and today and forever."

I know people may think, 'how many times did he need to get "played" before he is going to wake up?' The answer is, there is no time limit and when we are truly ready to see things the way they really are that is when we will wake up. God woke me up once I got to a certain point. My body was just tired. That day I could see clearer, I could think straight and I suddenly understood that this wasn't about me. I wanted to be married, she didn't. I wanted a family, she didn't. I finally realized that the fault did not lie with me and so I had nothing to correct. I began to read God's word and it became like a road map, telling me how to deal with my life. This was the best I had felt in years. I was happier at this point being single, then I had ever been in my marriage. It's sad to say, but true. I got up for work, smiling. I felt as though a weight had been lifted up off of me. I appreciated and loved my children and they appreciated and loved me. There was no more faking, pretending or phoniness in our household. Everyone and everything around me was authentic and real for the first time in a long time. My children were smiling because I was smiling more. I had the support of my family which I really needed. Their support was amazing. They offered no judgment, just general concern for my wellbeing and mental state. I didn't realize it but my marriage had kept me away from my family. I allowed my marriage to cause a separation between us, but I have closed that gap now. It feels good to come around close friends and family and smile and have them genuinely happy to see me happy. It feels good to have family cook for me and love me for who I am, not for what I have or for what I can do for them. Stay focused on getting to a happy place. The joy that I have the world didn't give it to me, so the world can't take it away.

LIFE LESSON #10

Proverbs 14:16-18 "One who is wise is cautious and turns away from evil, but a fool is reckless and careless. A man of quick temper acts foolishly, and a man of evil devices is hated. The simple inherit folly, but the prudent are crowned with knowledge."

I end this tale, taking full responsibility for my actions. I know some, or most, may say I was stupid…. but I wasn't stupid. I did what I thought a husband should do. I made some stupid decisions, this I can admit. Once I woke up and realized that I was just being used as a security blanket, then I understood my position. I know that to her, I was just a safe haven, but to me she was my wife. Now that it is over I can say I am truly happy. I have moved on, and have friends that care about me and only want to see me win. It feels good to not be used and abused but to be cherished and loved.

When I think back over my life, never would I have thought that I'd be where I am today. But this is where I am and I'm okay with that. It feels good to wake up in my own bed, in my space. I had to learn to break free from the negativity and live life from an honest and positive point of view. Learn to inhale all the good and exhale the BS.

CPSIA information can be obtained
at www.ICGtesting.com
Printed in the USA
LVOW03s1328130317
527004LV00003B/13/P

9 780692 841389